T0389933

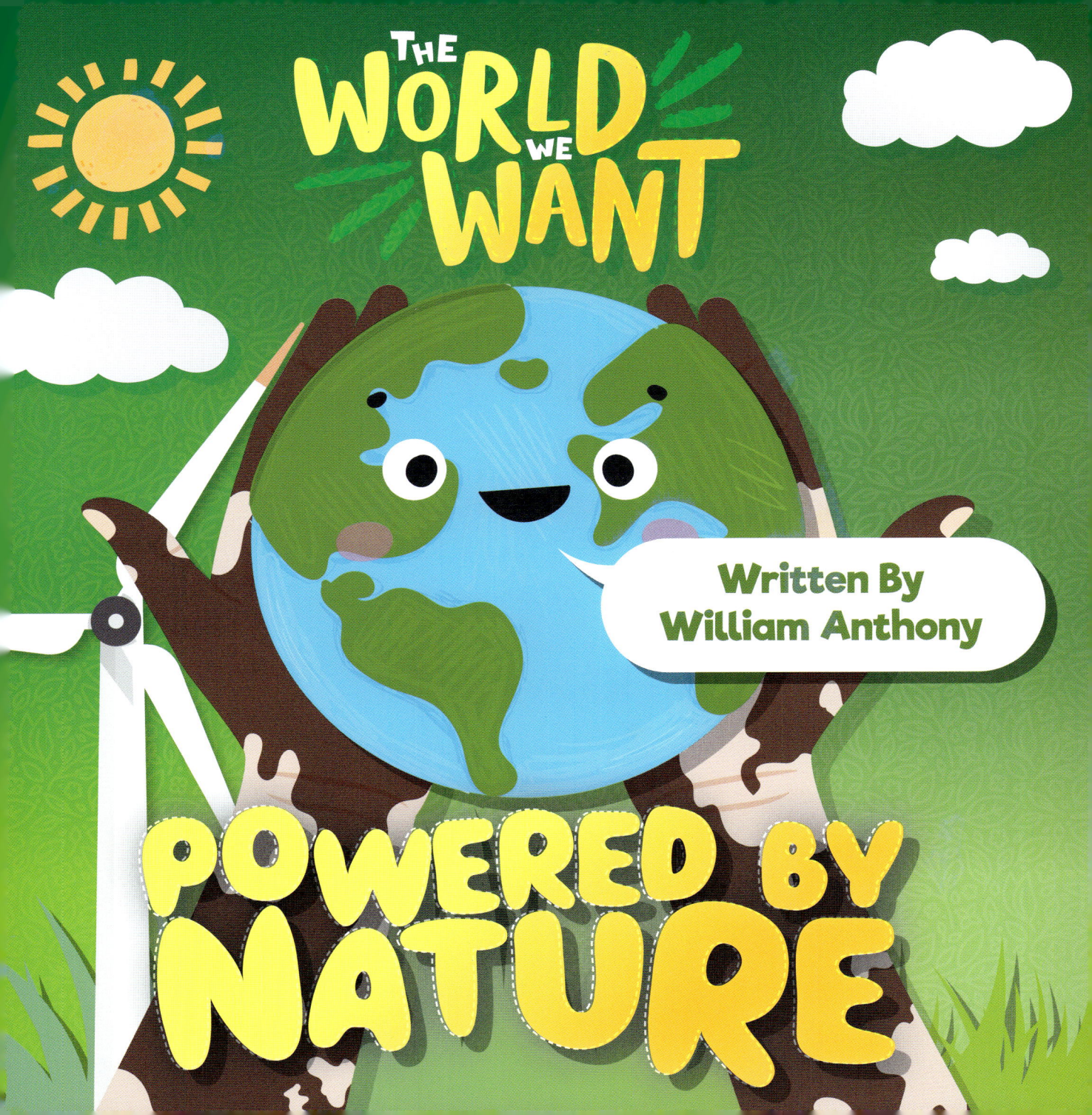

THE WORLD WE WANT

POWERED BY NATURE

Written By
William Anthony

Powered by Nature © 2024 BookLife Publishing
This edition is published by arrangement with BookLife Publishing

sales@northstareditions.com
888-417-0195

Library of Congress Control Number:
2025930770

ISBN
979-8-89359-336-5 (library bound)
979-8-89359-420-1 (paperback)
979-8-89359-366-2 (epub)
979-8-89359-390-7 (hosted ebook)

All facts, statistics, web addresses and URLs in this book were verified as valid and accurate at time of writing. No responsibility for any changes to external websites or references can be accepted by either the author or publisher.

Printed in the United States of America
Mankato, MN
092025

Written by:
William Anthony

Edited by:
Rebecca Phillips-Bartlett

Designed by:
Rob Delph

PHOTO CREDITS

CONTENTS

Page 4	No New Planet
Page 6	Power
Page 8	Eco-Friendly Power
Page 10	Wind
Page 14	Water
Page 18	The Sun
Page 22	Love Our Planet
Page 24	Glossary and Index

Words that look like this can be found in the glossary on page 24.

NO NEW PLANET

We live on a planet called Earth. We share Earth with lots of animals and plants. Humans, animals, and plants are all part of our planet's ecosystem.

CAN YOU SPOT WHERE YOU LIVE ON EARTH?

4

We must take care of Earth. Unfortunately, we don't have a new planet to go to if we damage this one. We need to work with nature to take care of the environment.

5

POWER

You use things that need power every day. Power is the _energy_ we get from our planet's _resources_. You need power to turn the TV on, charge your phone, and make your home warm.

Many resources will run out if we use too much of them. Coal, oil, and gas are three resources that will run out. Using these resources is also bad for our planet's air.

COAL BEING BURNED

OIL

GAS

ECO-FRIENDLY POWER

While some resources will eventually run out, others will not. Using these resources is much better for our planet. They include wind, water, and even the sun.

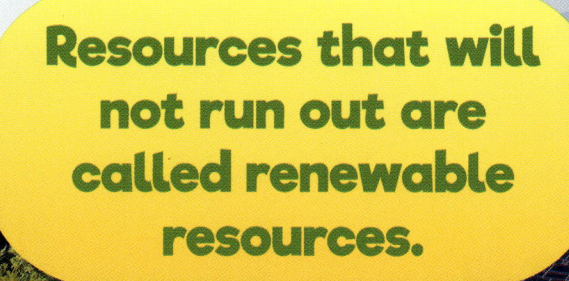

Resources that will not run out are called renewable resources.

When we use energy from wind, water, and the sun, we can keep our planet's air clean and safe. Many countries are trying to find ways to use renewable energy as much as possible.

WIND

Can you remember a day without any wind at all? Probably not! That is because wind will never run out. We can power our homes with it in a way that is safe for our planet.

Wind pushes large blades around on a wind turbine. These blades then turn a _motor_. This creates a type of energy called electricity, which we use for electronic items.

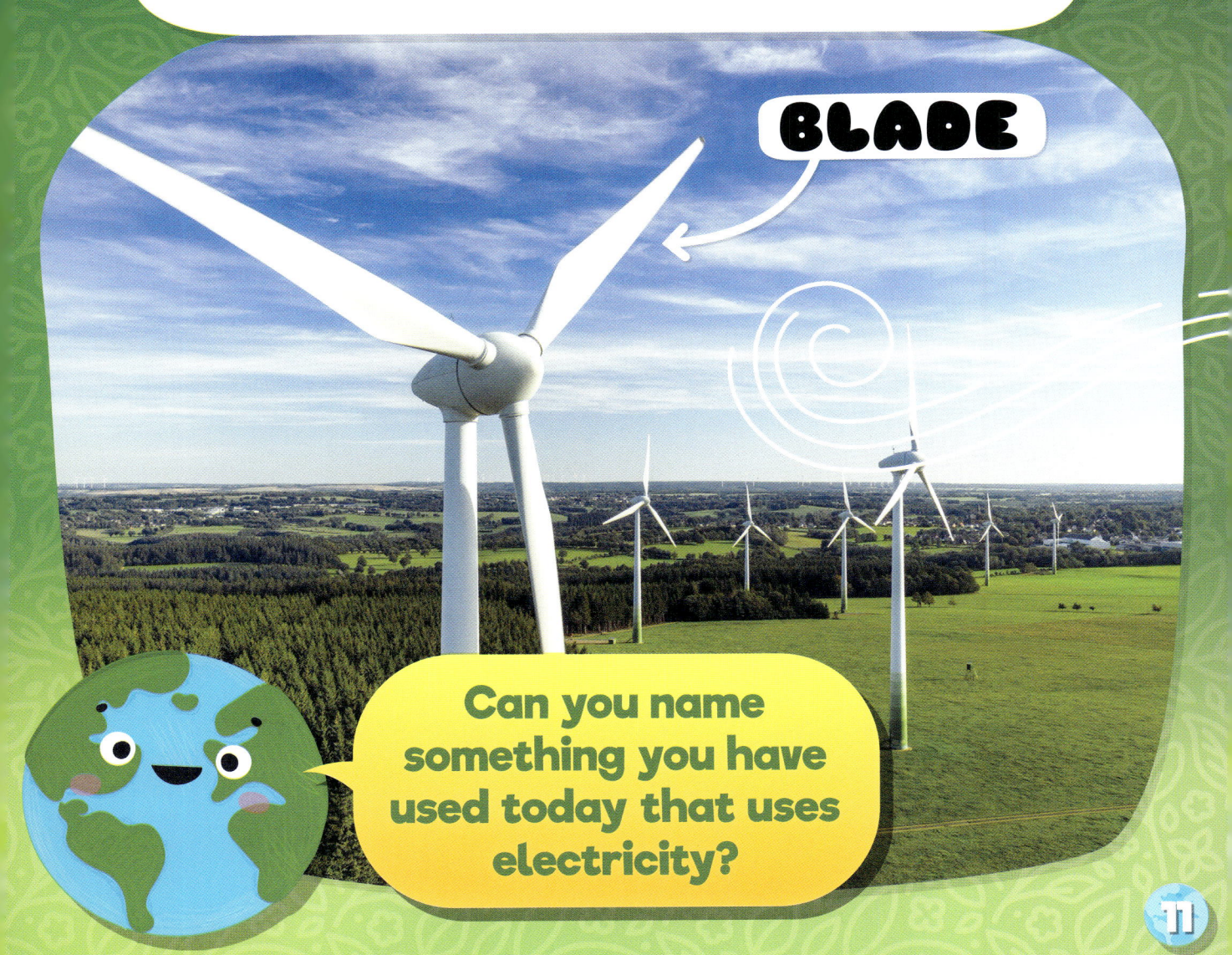

BLADE

Can you name something you have used today that uses electricity?

Let's try using wind power by making a paper windmill!

You will need:

- Scissors
- Pencil
- Ruler
- Square piece of paper
- Straw
- Pushpin
- Masking tape

1.

Draw a line on the paper from corner to corner to make a big cross.

2.

Cut along the lines from each corner halfway to the center.

3.

Fold the other sections into a small cross and put a pin through.

4.

With your adult's help, push the pin through the straw and add masking tape to protect your fingers.

5.

Take your windmill outside and watch it spin with the wind!

WATER

The water on our planet has always been here. It will never run out. We can use it to make power safely.

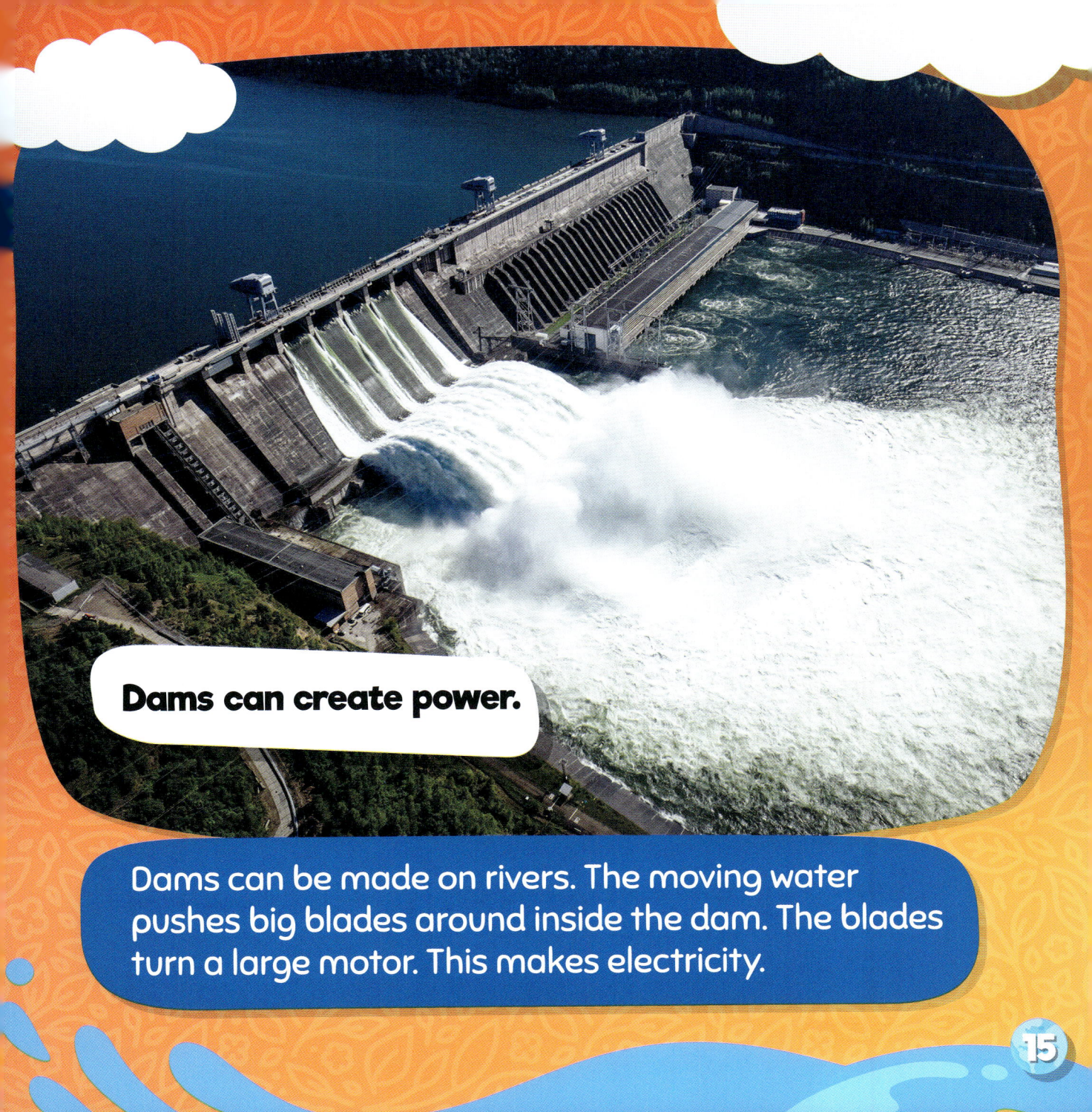

Dams can create power.

Dams can be made on rivers. The moving water pushes big blades around inside the dam. The blades turn a large motor. This makes electricity.

Let's _investigate_ the power of water!

1. Find three cups. Fill one with a tiny amount of water. Fill the next one about halfway. Fill the last one to the top. Take your cups outside.

2. Hold the emptiest cup out in front of you. Pour it onto the floor.

3. Repeat this with the half-full cup.

4. Repeat this with the full cup. Which splash was biggest?

The final splash should have been the biggest and most powerful because there was more water. Imagine how much power there is in an entire river!

THE SUN

The sun makes lots of light. It helps us see during the day. The sun's light will not run out. We can use energy from sunlight to safely create power for our planet.

The sun is always shining, even though you can't see it at night.

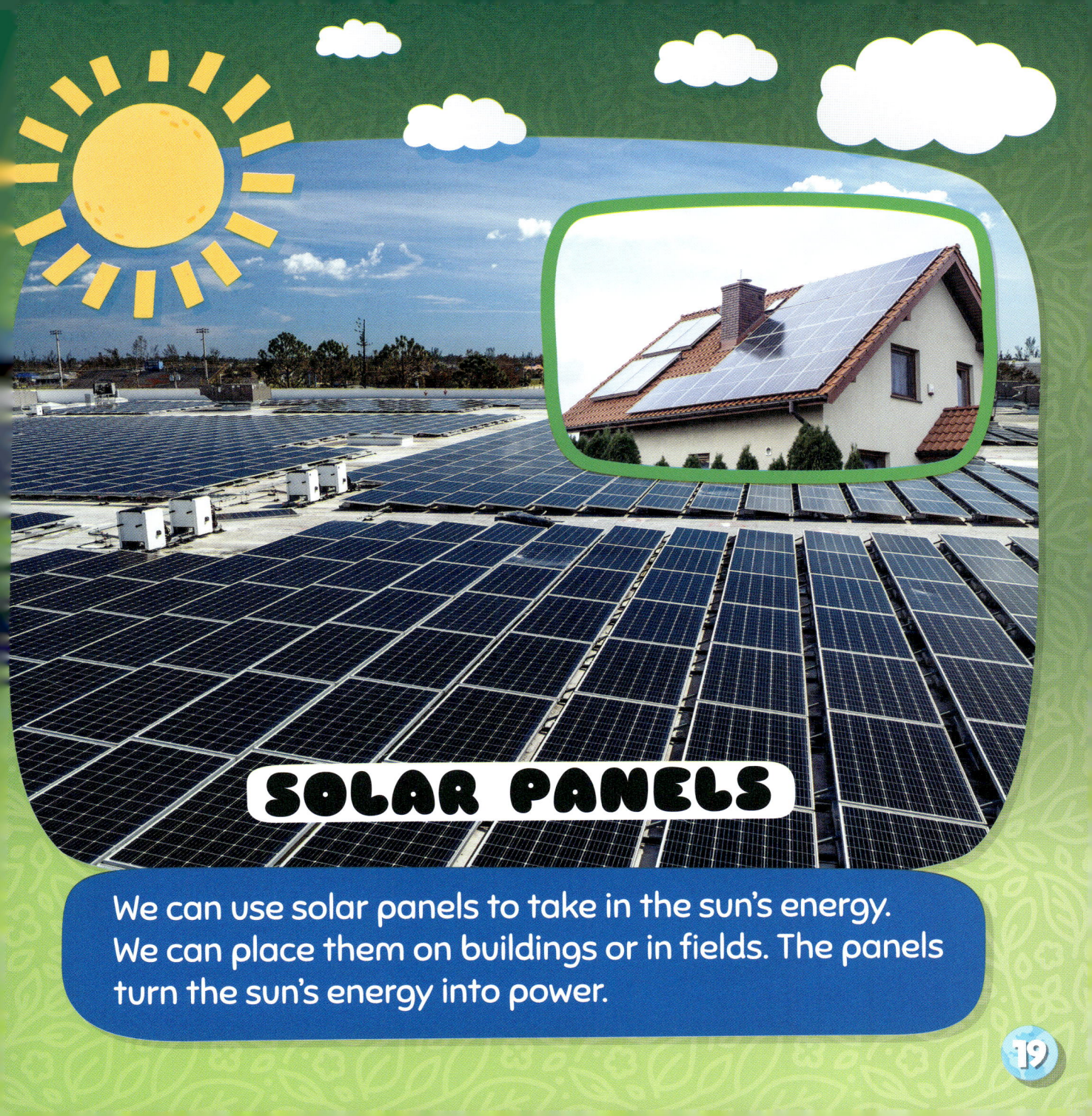

SOLAR PANELS

We can use solar panels to take in the sun's energy. We can place them on buildings or in fields. The panels turn the sun's energy into power.

Why are solar panels black instead of white? Let's find out!

1. Find a piece of black card and a piece of white card. Place them on the floor outside.

2. Ask an adult to find you two similar-sized ice cubes. Put one ice cube on each piece of card.

3.

Watch to see how long each ice cube takes to melt.

4.

The ice on the black card should melt faster than the ice on the white card.

5.

That means a black solar panel will take in more sunlight energy than a white one.

LOVE OUR PLANET

What actions will you take to look after our planet?

Our planet needs our help. How we use Earth's resources makes a big impact. People have found lots of ways to create power safely using nature.

Whether it is using wind, water, or the sun to power your home and everything in it, you can help. Together we can create the world we all want!

WIND

SUNLIGHT

WATER

GLOSSARY

ECOSYSTEM	everything that lives together in an environment
ENERGY	usable power that comes from heat, light, electricity, and other things
ENVIRONMENT	the surroundings that an animal, plant, or human lives in
INVESTIGATE	to try and find out about how something happens or works
MOTOR	a machine that produces power
NATURE	the world around us and everything in it that is not made by humans
RESOURCES	a supply of something that can be used when it is needed

INDEX

air	7, 9	**energy**	6, 9, 11, 18–19, 21	**solar panels**	19–21
blades	11, 15			**turbines**	11
dams	15			**windmills**	12–13
electricity	11, 15	**motors**	11, 15		